TAKING THE PAIN OUT OF MANAGING ONE DAY AT A TIME:

240 Bite-Size Strategies That Up Your Leadership Game

Taking the Pain Out of Managing One Day at a Time: 240 Bite-Size Strategies That Up Your Leadership Game

Fourth edition
ISBN-13: 978-0-692-63883-5
Library of Congress Control Number: 2011909684

HOW TO ORDER:
Copies may be ordered by contacting Leadership Cadence, LLC,
Quantity discounts available by calling +1-310-490-3730
or emailing info@leadershipcadence.com

To my clients,
who encourage
and challenge
me to be my
personal best
one day at a time.

Acknowledgments

I want to thank everyone who has helped with this book. A few dedicated individuals deserve special recognition: Anna Zetterholm, our fabulous Swedish maven, for keeping an unfalteringly positive attitude as we redesigned, reconstructed, and finally revamped the whole idea for this book; Jamie Wells, my wonderful executive assistant, for taking care of all the tedious office tasks every day, so I don't have to deal with them; and Nancy Flynn for exceptional editing assistance. Thank you to all my clients, old and new. By putting these tips to work over the decade, you have demonstrated that they deliver the promised results. Thank you for trying, testing, and stretching in the pursuit of excellence. Because of you, I love my job!

Introduction

This book began as a "cute little project," in which I envisioned myself writing a single management tip each morning, while leisurely sipping a cup of decaf at my favorite coffee shop. I pictured a Zen-like experience, with each idea flowing effortlessly. I imagined I would feel good about making time specifically for this enterprise.

Then reality hit. Each morning ran just a little bit later than the previous day. Before I knew it, I was giving priority to checking email and other routine, but seemingly urgent, tasks. The coffee shop visit became a seemingly unattainable dream, and time just disappeared before my eyes. Does this sound familiar?

One day I realized that, if I didn't make this book a priority, I would never get it done (and I'm one of those people who can't let an unfinished project go). My only option was to get real about setting aside clearly defined intervals to work on it—not a few stolen minutes a day, but dedicated blocks of time. I set myself a completion deadline of three months.

At first glance, writing 240 tips didn't seem like a huge undertaking. But, I soon realized that I could write for only about two hours a day, while still maintaining my creativity and focus. I could produce about 20 tips in that time. That meant that I needed to set aside 12 two-hour slots on my calendar to finish the project. My first thought was that it wasn't going to happen. How could I free up that much time over such a short period?

I started by taking small steps. I asked my assistant to leave my calendar clear before noon on Fridays. To further eliminate distractions, I decided to go to a coffee shop that didn't offer Internet access. Twelve weeks later, this book was ready! It is amazing what you can accomplish by getting clear about what you want to achieve, aligning your resources accordingly, and staying committed in thought and action.

The tips that follow are management strategies, similar to the ones I used to create this book. I learned some of them from clients and some from personal trial and error. They may appear overly simple or "small" on first reading, but that is intentional. As an executive coach and corporate trainer, I know that most of us can process or work on only one change at a time. When we try to do more, we just don't follow through.

If you have ever tried to lose or gain weight, you know how challenging it can be to stick to a new habit. If you want to lose 50 pounds, for example, you may feel overwhelmed by the thought of dieting for several months. But if you focus on just one modification, such as eliminating snacks or eating one healthy meal each day, then it is a lot easier to reach your goal. While you may be able to lose 10 pounds a week through starvation, this radical approach is also more likely to induce overeating and actually cause a weight gain. Remember, little steps add up. Indeed, one small step after another is the only way to sustain change over the long haul.

This book isn't going to miraculously change you or how you work, but it will help you move one step closer each day to becoming a more effective manager. If you commit to taking one of these action steps daily, you will be amazed at how much you will accomplish and how many goals you will reach over the next year.

The format of this book is consistent with my organization's to-the-point philosophy. It provides short and parctical tips along with inspirational quotes and resource material to support you in becoming an exceptional manager.

One of my favorite quotes from legendary business and personal development expert Jim Rohn is, "Don't wish it were easier; wish you were better." It reminds me that, with effort and commitment, I can always improve myself and advance my goals.

Let me know which strategies help move you forward.

Enjoy!

Jonrika Jagnmmon

P.S. If you are wondering why this book contains 240 tips, rather than 365, I based my count on total number of work days in a year. Most business professionals work five days a week, 52 weeks a year, minus three weeks of vacation and holiday time. That equals work days - and 240 bite-size strategies.

How to Get the Most From This Book:

The truth is, if you randomly pick just one tip in this book and act on it, you will improve your management skills and see measurable results. So imagine if you commit to acting on, let's say, half, or 120, of these tips. Imagine the type of manager you will become in just six months!

The key to getting the most from this book is to read each tip, quote, or question, and then take time to write down an action step in the "Today I will…" box on each page. Keep these action steps short and concise.

If you are really committed to developing your management skills, I suggest you:

1. Schedule a 5-10 minute daily meeting with yourself on your calendar. Name it, "Management Development" and commit yourself to it. I find that early in the morning, before I check email and start working, is a great time for me because I am less likely to be interrupted or distracted.

2. Each day review one tip, and one tip only! Remember, this is more like a marathon than a sprint. If you over-commit early on, you are likely to lose steam as you move along.

3. Take one small action step that you know, without a shadow of a doubt, you can implement or act upon. If you can't say "yes" without reservation, the step is probably too big. Break it down into the smallest piece possible and act on that.

4. Pick a specific milestone ("after seven action steps" or "after the first month," for example) and celebrate your management-development accomplishments. Treat yourself to a nice lunch or leave early one day to give yourself a pat on the back. After all, making positive changes calls for a celebration! Remember, "That which you focus on grows."

Following these steps will help you move forward faster and with more powerful results. Are you ready to get started?

−1−

Schedule Time for Strategic Thinking

Allocate 30 minutes on your calendar this week to begin mapping out your goals. Begin by establishing larger goals and then assign smaller "sub-goals."

Today I will...

Ask Your Team to Set Aside Time

Ask your team to schedule 30 minutes for strategic thinking and planning. When your entire team is aligned with your goals, you will get a lot more accomplished.

Today I will...

−3−

Set Up a Strategic Brainstorming Meeting

Schedule a one-hour strategic brainstorming meeting with your team to discuss goals, desires, and accountability. Make it a habit to conduct these sessions monthly.

Today I will...

-4-

Connect With a Quote

*"Managers who clearly communicate their
expectations, goals, and visions lead more effectively."*

– Jessika Magnusson

What one thing can you do today to embrace this concept?

Today I will...

−5−

SMARTify Your Goals

Make sure your goals are **S**pecific, **M**easurable, **A**ttainable, **R**elevant, and **T**imed. Ask yourself, "If others read this goal, could they accomplish it and get the result I expect?"

Today I will...

DAY

-6-

Identify Your Key People

For each goal you establish, identify at least one person who must be part of the process in order for it to be accomplished. Schedule time to meet with that person to map out a plan.

Today I will...

DAY

−7−

Today I'm Ready For...

Complete the sentence above, focusing on the positive actions, thoughts, and behaviors you want to embrace today.

Today I'm ready for...

-8-

Make Sure Your People Are SMART

Meet with at least one of your direct reports or team members and share the SMART acronym. Ask that person to share a goal with you and work together to make it **S**pecific, **M**easurable, **A**ttainable, **R**elevant, and **T**imed.

Today I will...

-9-

SMARTïfy Your Life

Use the SMART principle in your everyday life. Get in the habit of asking, "When do I need to get back to you?" "If I do X, will your expectations be met?" "Is it reasonable for us to expect X in return?"

Today I will...

Connect With a Quote

*"Effective leadership is putting first things first.
Effective management is discipline, carrying it out."*

– Stephen Covey

What do you want to be more disciplined about?

Today I will…

–11–

Establish Your
Non-Negotiables

Write down at least one non-negotiable management standard. These usually are connected to the values and principles by which you work. For example, "We start all meetings on time regardless of who is in attendance," or "I expect all team members to address issues directly with the person they are challenged by."

Today I will...

Share Your
Non-Negotiables

Share at least one of your non-negotiable standards with your team members. Ask them for feedback and double-check for any confusion. Once clear, hold team members accountable to that standard immediately from that meeting forward.

Today I will…

−13−

Today I'm Ready For...

Complete the sentence above, focusing on the positive actions, thoughts, and behaviors you want to embrace today.

Today I'm ready for...

−14−

Ask Your Team for Their Non-Negotiables

Teach your team members to establish up to three non-negotiable standards to which they will hold their direct reports accountable. Offer feedback and support.

Today I will…

−15−

Connect With a Quote

*"Effective management always means
asking the right question."*

– Robert Heller

What questions do you need to ask in order to get
the answers you want?

Today I will...

DAY
−16−

Get Clear About
Your Strengths

List at least two management strengths you possess, and
identify one action step you will take today to maximize one (or
both) of them.

Today I will...

–17–

Share Your Strengths With Others

Offer to share one of your management strengths with at least one other person. Notice how they respond to your offer.

Today I will...

−18−

Today I'm Ready For...

Complete the sentence above, focusing on the positive actions, thoughts, and behaviors you want to embrace today.

Today I'm ready for...

−19−

Check in on Another Person's Strengths

Ask at least one other person with whom you work frequently to share a strength that individual possesses. Check to see if this is a strength that would compliment your set of skills. If so, ask for permission to "borrow" the strength in the future.

Today I will...

-20-

Embrace and Celebrate Your Strengths

Spend today basking in the amazing qualities that make you who you are! Enjoy your strengths and celebrate how great you are. Kids are exceptional at this. Embrace your inner child for just one day and enjoy the results.

Today I will...

Connect With a Quote

"Good management consists in showing average people how to do the work of superior people."

– John D. Rockefeller

How can you show your team
to get superior performance?

Today I will…

−22−

Accept Your Flaws

You are not perfect and neither is anyone else. Embrace your imperfections and identify one person on your team or a peer who may have a strength you lack. Rely on that person to help you deliver exceptional work.

Today I will…

−23−

Minimize Your Most Pervasive Weaknesses

While it may be hard to accept, we all have them. Don't over-focus on your weaknesses, but commit to minimizing your most pervasive one. For example, if you are tardy in responding to phone calls, assign one day this week for returning phone calls in a timely manner.

Today I will...

−24−

Connect With a Quote

"I think management is about just that—
managing people via man-to-man skills."

– Stuart Pearce

How can you get more connected to
your team members today?

Today I will…

–25–

Get Clear

We often think that we are clear about what we want or ask of others. The truth is that most of us are not as clear as we think we are. Ask someone to paraphrase
a statement you have made, then check your
"clarity quotient."

Today I will...

Today I'm Ready For...

Complete the sentence above, focusing on the positive actions, thoughts, and behaviors you want to embrace today.

Today I'm ready for...

-27-

Be More Direct

Most managers are not as direct as they think they are. Being direct without being blunt, harsh, or dictatorial takes practice. Challenge yourself today to make one direct statement to someone with whom you work. Watch that person's response or feedback.

Today I will...

–28–

Stop Skirting Around the Issue

Effective managers know how to clearly identify a situation and speak directly to it without skirting around the issue. Practice being clear and direct in order to amp up your management volume.

Today I will...

-29-

Practice Speaking From the Heart

When we get good at speaking from the heart, we communicate the truth. If we want to resolve issues, speaking the truth is the only way to go. Remember to do so tactfully.

Today I will...

-30-

Embrace the Truth

It is sometimes hard to speak and live in the truth. We don't want to hurt other people's feelings, and we don't want to be "bad" managers. When we communicate the truth in a way that opens up communication, we are truly powerful. Who do you need to speak the truth to today?

Today I will...

–31–

Connect With a Quote

"A manager is an assistant to his men."

– Thomas J. Watson

What can you do to assist your team today?

Today I will…

−32−

Compliment Someone

When we compliment others, we offer them a positive emotion.
We also tend to feel good when we give of ourselves. As
managers we can get so stuck on what needs to be improved
that we forget to appreciate what is. Offer someone a
compliment today.

Today I will...

-33-

Today I'm Ready For...

Complete the sentence above, focusing on the positive actions, thoughts, and behaviors you want to embrace today.

Today I'm ready for...

-34-

Get Clear About What You Want

Set aside 15 minutes this week to get clear about what you want. When you increase your clarity, you will be able to communicate and delegate what you want more effectively.

Today I will...

DAY

-35-

Get Clear About
Who You Are

Spend 10 minutes today contemplating who you are as a manager. Ask, *What matters to me? On what am I not willing to negotiate?* When you are clear about who you are, others can more easily meet your needs.

Today I will…

Connect With a Quote

*"A manager is not a person who can do the work
better than his men; he is a person who can get his
men to do the work better than he can."*

– Frederick W. Smith

What do you need to delegate today?

Today I will...

-37-

Stop and Start What You Are Doing

Stop what you are doing and consider if this is the right thing to be working on right now. Ask yourself if there is a better way to do this task. Should you be delegating it to free up time? If you are convinced it is the right time and the right task, begin the activity again.

Today I will...

-38-

Today I'm Ready For...

Complete the sentence above, focusing on the positive actions, thoughts, and behaviors you want to embrace today.

Today I'm ready for...

-39-

Eliminate Confusion

Communicating clearly will eliminate unnecessary confusion. Set aside 10 minutes today to review an assignment or situation that appears to bring confusion. What do you need to do to clarify the situation? What are you doing to contribute to the lack of clarity?

Today I will...

-40-

Take a Break

Leave your desk and get out of the office. Spend 45 minutes away from your office today. Grab a coffee or lunch. Walk around the building. Get some air. It is amazing how much creativity you can gain from getting out of your rut.

Today I will...

-41-

Connect With a Quote

"Good management is the art of making problems so interesting and their solutions so constructive that everyone wants to get to work and deal with them."

– Paul Hawken

How can you transform your team's obstacles into interesting problems to solve?

Today I will...

−42−

Today I'm Ready For...

Complete the sentence above, focusing on the
positive actions, thoughts, and behaviors you want
to embrace today.

Today I'm ready for...

-43-

Separate Excuses
from Mishaps

If people continually seem confused by the tasks you delegate, and you don't see consistent, satisfactory results, ask yourself these questions: Was I crystal clear about what I expected? Did I leave any opportunity for misunderstanding when I delegated this activity? If so, you can correct the mishap. If you were clear, you probably have an excuse to address.

Today I will...

-44-

Check In With Your Peeps Today

If you are like most managers, you may forget to check in with your team members to see how they are doing. Connect with at least one person today. This powerful in-the-moment strategy lets your peeps know you care.

Today I will...

DAY

-45-

Connect With a Quote

"An employee's motivation is a direct result of the sum of interactions with his or her manager."

– Bob Nelson

What do you need to do today to create a 15-minute conversation with at least one of your team members?

Today I will…

-46-

Use Upfront Agreements

An upfront agreement is something you determine prior to engaging in an activity or project. It allows you to address potential issues before they happen and establish an action plan for handling them effectively. Establish one upfront agreement today that you anticipate using with your team, boss, or peers in the future.

Today I will...

−47−

Learn Something New Today

Set aside 30 minutes to read or learn something new today. Pick a resource (book, article, webpage) and identify one concept or idea to use with your team. Avoid trying to tackle resources that require more than two hours of dedicated time. Chances are you will get too busy and won't get to it. Small steps add up!

Today I will...

-48-

Connect With a Quote

*"Yesterday is gone. Tomorrow has not yet come.
We have only today. Let us begin."*

— Mother Teresa

What do you want to do today to improve, develop,
or grow as a manager or leader?

Today I will...

-49-

Important vs. Urgent Inventory

Draw an L on a piece of paper. At the top corner of the vertical L write *Important*. At the end of the horizontal L write *Urgent*. Write your activities on the grid and see how many are both urgent AND important. What can you do today to change the division from important–urgent to important-not urgent?

Today I will...

−50−

Today I'm Ready For...

Complete the sentence above, focusing on the positive actions, thoughts, and behaviors you want to embrace today.

Today I'm ready for...

−51−

Commit to Being Great
at One Thing Today

Jim Collins, author of *Good to Great* says, "Good is the enemy of great." Pick one thing to be great at today. It could be returning all emails within 24 hours or completing an excellent report. Push your limits and don't stop until you know you are doing your best.

Today I will...

Delegate What You Are Good At

Only spend time doing what you are truly great at. Delegate the rest. If someone else is exceptional at
what you are good at, that individual will do it with less effort and more enthusiasm. What can you delegate today that allow you to work on things that maximize your talents?

Today I will…

-53-

Connect With a Quote

"The first rule of management is delegation. Don't try and do everything yourself because you can't."

– Anthea Turner

What do you need to delegate to someone else in order to avoid doing everything yourself?

Today I will...

DAY

−54−

Front-load Your Messages

Are you communicating the most important things
first in emails and other written communications?
If not, begin front-loading - state your key message(s) right
away.

Today I will...

Complete Only One
Thing Today

Your to-do list is probably pretty long, but for one day, give yourself permission to complete only one thing on your list. If you have time left over, then by all means, continue knocking things off, as long as that one thing
is complete.

Today I will...

–56–

Today I'm Ready For...

Complete the sentence above, focusing on the positive actions, thoughts, and behaviors you want to embrace today.

Today I'm ready for...

−57−

Pick One Goal and Work It

Take a look at the goals you have set for the year. Pick one that you are excited about and set aside one hour today to devote to it.

Today I will...

DAY
-58-

Connect With a Quote

"You can't be a great manager unless you are a great communicator. It's not about how much they like you. It's about how effective you are in their eyes."

– The No Frills No Fluff® Management Skills Program

What can you work on today to be a
more effective communicator?

Today I will…

Are Your Points Coming Across?

If not, what do you need to do or change to ensure that others hear your messages as you intend them?

Today I will…

-60-

Know Your Communication Strengths

Set aside 10 minutes to consider your biggest communication asset. Ask yourself, "How often do I use it?""If I maximized it, what results would I see?"

Today I will...

-61-

Repeat That Back to Me

This may sound like an over-used strategy, but it really works. Ask your team to repeat what you say, and then check for possible miscommunication.

Today I will...

-62-

Today I'm Ready For...

Complete the sentence above, focusing on the
positive actions, thoughts, and behaviors you want
to embrace today.

Today I'm ready for...

-63-

Remove Foot From Mouth

We all do it at some point. We say the wrong thing at the wrong time. Take ownership and apologize. People appreciate managers who are self-aware.

Today I will...

DAY
-64-

Connect With a Quote

"Bad news isn't bad wine. It doesn't improve with age."

– Colin Powell

How comfortable and tactful are you
at delivering bad news?

Today I will…

DAY
-65-

A Miscommunication is an Opportunity

Take the time to clarify and correct miscommunications, allowing for a deeper and more effective relationship to form.

Today I will...

-66-

Leverage Your Communication Strengths

If you are a great listener, highlight this trait to create deeper connections with others. If you are a great presenter, offer your services to someone who may be struggling. Spend today focusing on your strengths.

Today I will...

-67-

Flex Your Style

When you adapt your communication style to fit the styles of others, you create win-win relationships. Take a moment today to try flexing your style. Notice if it is challenging or easy.

Today I will...

-68-

Continue That Thought...

Avoid interrupting others when they speak. Practice saying, "Please continue that thought," when you get the urge to interrupt. Chances are, the other person has some great ideas and input to share.

Today I will...

-69-

Today I'm Ready For...

Complete the sentence above, focusing on the positive actions, thoughts, and behaviors you want to embrace today.

Today I'm ready for...

−70−

My Core Behavioral Style Is...

If you already know, great. Remember that your style may differ from others. If you don't know, use the bonus resource below to complete a quick self-scorer. The better you know yourself, the more effective you will be with others.

Today I will...

-71-

Connect With a Quote

"It's not what you say, but how you say it that matters."

– Anonymous

This popular quote makes a lot of sense.
What do you need to change or modify about
your communication style to develop your
"how you say it" skills?

Today I will...

-72-

What's Your Core Style?

Ask someone else to share their core behavioral style with you. Practice flexing your style to meet that person halfway. If you feel brave, ask your boss to share his or her style with you, and start building a powerful relationship with him or her.

Today I will...

-73-

Do a "Listening Inventory"

Ask a person you trust to rate your listening skills on a scale of 1-10 (1 being poor; 10 being exceptional). Ask for feedback on the score. If less than a 10, make a commitment to improve. If a 10, ask another person!

Today I will...

Connect With a Quote

*"When you're not caught up in being right,
then you have the ability to listen when an issue comes up—
and I mean really listen."*

– Harry Kraemer

If you didn't feel the need to be right, how would you
approach the situation differently?

Today I will…

−75−

Meet in Person

Replace one email communication with an in-person visit. Did you notice any changes in the communication? Do you feel more connected? Were you able to avoid possible miscommunications? Use this strategy once a month to develop stronger relationships.

Today I will...

-76-

Today I'm Ready For...

Complete the sentence above, focusing on the positive actions, thoughts, and behaviors you want to embrace today.

Today I'm ready for...

-77-

Manage Your Email

I know. This may seem like an overwhelming statement.
Try email boundary-setting for one day. Respond to email
only three times throughout the day, setting a timeline for
responses.

Today I will...

Connect With a Quote

"For example, I was discussing the use of email and how impersonal it can be, how people will now email someone across the room rather than go and talk to them. But I don't think this is laziness; I think it is a conscious decision people are making to save time."

– Margaret J. Wheatley

Are you using email for the right reason?
Is there a more effective way to communicate?

Today I will...

-79-

Use the Three-Email Rule

If your primary message hasn't been clearly communicated after three exchanges, pick up the
phone or visit the recipient in person. This will save time and prevent future email miscommunications.

Today I will…

–80–

Take an IM Break

If you use Instant Messaging (IM) for work, turn it off for fifteen minutes to one hour during the day. Notice how you feel knowing you won't be pinged. What will you do with time otherwise spend responding to IMs?

Today I will...

-81-

Take a Facebook Break

If you are able to access Facebook at work, stop using it! This huge time-waster eats away at your energy and focus.

Today I will...

-82-

Create "Interruption Free" Zones

Research shows that it takes about 15 minutes to recover from an interruption. If you have more than four interruptions in one hour, you are spending twice as long working as you need to. Consider what you would do with this time if you were not interrupted so frequently. Develop a strategy to let people know that you need uninterrupted time - and when you need it.

Today I will...

Today I'm Ready For...

Complete the sentence above, focusing on the positive actions, thoughts, and behaviors you want to embrace today.

Today I'm ready for...

-84-

Write Like a Pro

Despite what you (and many Gen Xers and other young employees) may think, people judge you based on your written communication. Avoid slang, abbreviations, and shortcuts when writing to anyone above age 19. Commit to proper mechanics (grammar, punctuation, capitalization) and effective writing style.

Today I will...

DAY

-85-

Connect With a Quote

"Saying nothing...sometimes says the most."

– Emily Dickinson

How can you say more by saying less?

Today I will...

-86-

"Your Preferred Communication Style?"

Ask your boss and staff what their preferred communication styles are. Do they like it short and sweet? Do they prefer a lot of detail? Do they want the conversation to be fun and exciting? Do they prefer a slow and steady pace? Once you know the answer, you can begin to flex your style.

Today I will...

Find a Proofreader

Ask a colleague or hire an external resource to proofread important documents. Don't let your boss catch your unintended mistakes.

Today I will...

Audit Your Emails

Take a look at your emails and ask yourself, "Would I be okay if the president of my company read this email?" "Are my emails clear and concise?" "Do I hide behind email to address issues I should handle on the phone or in person?"

Today I will...

-89-

Connect With a Quote

"It seemed rather incongruous that in a society of super-sophisticated communication, we often suffer from a shortage of listeners."

– Erma Bombeck

What low-tech communication technique can you use to up your communication skills?

Today I will...

-90-

Catch Your People Doing Things Right

Look for opportunities to give positive feedback. When your team is in sync and things are going well, show them you notice. Small and consistent acknowledgments go a long way.

Today I will...

-91-

Today I'm Ready For...

Complete the sentence above, focusing on the positive actions, thoughts, and behaviors you want to embrace today.

Today I'm ready for...

-92-

Find a Communication Mentor

Study a person you admire and copy one of that individual's communication strategies today.

Today I will...

-93-

Take Something Back

If you said or did something you regret, take it back. Let the person know you regret what you said and apologize for being insensitive, rude, or blunt.

Today I will...

-94-

Stand Up to Dominant Communicators

Don't let dominant people push you around. Hold your ground politely and share objective details that support your decision or stand. They may not enjoy your pushing back, but they are likely to respect it.

Today I will...

-95-

Put Some Sparkle In It

Communicators who are positive and upbeat respond well to exciting words, energizing messages, and laughter. Practice putting some "sparkles" in your communication this week.

Today I will...

Connect With a Quote

"The imperative is to define what is right and do it."

– Barbara Jordan

What do you need to clarify, in order to determine
what is right for you as a manager?

Today I will…

-97-

Offer Step-by-Step Solutions

People who prefer a slower, steadier pace respond well to solutions that are outlined in clear steps.

Today I will...

-98-

Get Organized

Compliant communicators prefer to interact with others who come well-prepared and have compiled organized data.

Today I will...

-99-

Today I'm Ready For...

Complete the sentence above, focusing on the positive actions, thoughts, and behaviors you want to embrace today.

Today I'm ready for...

-100-

Sharpen Your Skills for Life

Being a great communicator expands beyond work. Commit to becoming an excellent communicator in all aspects of your life and seek out opportunities to sharpen your skills.

Today I will...

-101-

Love Your Imperfections

This may seem a bit daunting at first. If so, start by simply learning to like them. If we accept our imperfections, we begin to make progress. Remember, if they wanted to hire perfection, they would have bought a robot. Sometimes your imperfections are perfect for the occasion.

Today I will...

Accept Others' Imperfections

You're not perfect, and neither are they. Sort out which imperfections you are able to manage, and which you can help others overcome. If certain imperfections consistently affect the team's performance negatively, you may want to consider making a staffing change.

Today I will...

Connect With a Quote

"Successful managers consistently give others the responsibility and authority to act on their behalf."

– Jessika Magnusson

What do you need to give up today in order to give someone else authority to act on your behalf?

Today I will...

-104-

Do a Delegation-
Strength Inventory

Make a list of at least three delegation strengths
that help you get things done. Review your list, considering
whether or not you are maximizing
those strengths currently.

Today I will...

DAY

–105–

Delegate What Drives You Nuts

Most of us hold onto things we should delegate, because we feel only we can do them correctly. Delegate something today that you just don't want
to do. If you can't delegate the entire activity, pick just one part of it, and make your life a little bit easier.

Today I will...

−106−

Stop Doing Things for Them

Managers often end up doing things that others should be doing. If you fall into the "doing it for them" trap, practice asking your people these questions: "By when will you get back to me with an update?" "How will you ensure that we get the outcome we agreed to?" This will help you from completing or taking on work you have already delegated.

Today I will…

–107–

Today I'm Ready For...

Complete the sentence above, focusing on the positive actions, thoughts, and behaviors you want to embrace today.

Today I'm ready for...

-108-

Set Aside Time to Prioritize

The biggest mistake managers make is that they don't take time to prioritize. If you don't have a clear sense of what needs to be accomplished, it is really hard to delegate to others. Set aside 15 minutes today to get organized.

Today I will...

–109–

Create an Easy-to-Use Delegation System

You don't need advanced spreadsheets or documents to delegate effectively. The key is to use one system, not several different notepads or documents. List the activities, assign priority codes, and begin to delegate.

Today I will...

Connect With a Quote

*"Don't be a time manager; be a priority manager.
Cut your major goals into bite-sized pieces.
Each small priority or requirement on the way to
ultimate goal become a mini goal in itself."*

– Denis Waitley

What activity do you need to cut into smaller pieces
to make sure it gets done?

Today I will...

−111−

I Don't Delegate Because…

Fill in the rest of this sentence, then look at your answers. Most people recognize that they don't delegate because a variety of fears holds them back. How would your workday look if you didn't let these fears prevent you from delegating?

Today I will…

Create a Delegation "Can" List

Audit your activities. Identify at least one thing that takes up about two hours a week. What you would do with those two hours if you instead delegated that activity?

Today I will...

-113-

Identify Your Delegation "Can't" List

Make a list of at least three activities that you can't delegate. If you spent more focused time on those activities, and less time focused on activities that
could be delegated, how much time would you save each week?

Today I will...

−114−

Today I'm Ready For...

Complete the sentence above, focusing on the
positive actions, thoughts, and behaviors you want
to embrace today.

Today I'm ready for...

−115−

Use the 3-Ds

The 3-Ds exercise is a great strategy for getting organized. Create three piles and put the following stickers on the respective piles. "Do It." "Dump It." "Delegate It." Take your current projects, unread mail, piles of work, and begin sorting.

Today I will...

Connect With a Quote

"Surround yourself with the best people you can find, delegate authority, and don't interfere."

– Ronald Reagan

How can you make sure you don't interfere with your delegated activities?

Today I will…

−117−

Ask What Motivates Your Peeps

If you don't know what motivates your peeps, it's hard to delegate things that get them fired up. Ask at least one of your team members why he comes to work. Use this information to help delegate things your peeps are motivated to do.

Today I will...

–118–

Assess Your Team's Motivators

There are several assessment tools that managers can use to help identify what drives and motivates their people. The more you know, the easier your job will be. Ask your team members what motivates them.

Today I will...

-119-

Correct Delegation Mishaps

When we delegate something and don't generate the results we expect, we need to consistently review possible delegation mishaps or mistakes. Ask yourself, was I crystal clear about what I wanted back, and did we agree on a deadline for this activity? If not, remember to do so next time.

Today I will...

DAY

−120−

Become a Deadline Hawk

Review your delegated activities and scan them for clearly articulated deadlines. If they are unclear or missing, go back and establish deadlines to help others stay on task and deliver what you want.

Today I will...

-121-

Today I'm Ready For...

Complete the sentence above, focusing on the positive actions, thoughts, and behaviors you want to embrace today.

Today I'm ready for...

Connect With a Quote

"Management by objectives works if you first think through your objectives. Ninety percent of the time you haven't."

– Peter Drucker

How much time do you set aside to
think through your objectives each week?

Today I will…

-123-

Stop Accepting Excuses

If you have delegated activities using clear deadlines and expectations but don't get the results you are looking for, begin addressing excuses. Decide what you will do if the behavior doesn't change. Excuses reinforce poor performance.

Today I will...

−124−

Delegate Upward

Review your delegation list and identify at least one activity
you can delegate to your boss. Consider his/
her strengths and ask for help on tasks that utilize
those strengths.

Today I will...

-125-

Delegate Sideways

Your peers can be powerful helpers during time crunches and for specialized projects. Ask peers to help you with tasks in which they have expertise. Promise to do the same for them in the future.

Today I will...

–126–

Send Someone in Your Place

You probably don't need to be in every meeting you are invited to attend. Ask the organizer to clarify the reasons for your attendance and send someone in your place if possible.

Today I will…

−127−

Today I'm Ready For...

Complete the sentence above, focusing on the positive actions, thoughts, and behaviors you want to embrace today.

Today I'm ready for...

-128-

Tap Into Hidden Talents

Ask your team members to identify at least one strength or skill they have outside of work. Review
these skills and brainstorm opportunities for tapping into these strengths at work.

Today I will…

-129-

Connect With a Quote

"People are definitely a company's greatest asset. It doesn't make any difference whether the product is cars or cosmetics. A company is only as good as the people it keeps."

– Mary Kay Ash

Who are the great people on your team?
Who needs development? Who should leave?

Today I will…

-130-

Know What it Takes to Do Their Job

Do you know what it takes to do your team members' jobs? If not, schedule a 15-minute meeting this week to learn more about what goes into getting their work done. You may discover ways to help them be more effective or for you to delegate more activities to free
up your time.

Today I will...

−131−

Use Check-ins

Establishing a check-in date for each delegated activity helps you avoid delegation mishaps. For each delegated activity, set a date where you will check in. Ask your team members to share updates on the activities. It's not your job to check in on them.

Today I will...

-132-

Set Deadlines

Make it a habit to always set deadlines for each activity you delegate. Review your recently delegated activities and see what you may have missed.

Today I will...

-133-

Know Your Drop Deadlines

The drop deadline is *your* deadline. The deadline you communicate to your team members should be a few days prior to yours in order to address possible mishaps or mistakes.

Today I will...

-134-

Today I'm Ready For...

Complete the sentence above, focusing on the positive actions, thoughts, and behaviors you want to embrace today.

Today I'm ready for...

−135−

Connect With a Quote

"Never tell people how to do things. Tell them what to do, and they will surprise you with their ingenuity."

− George S. Patton

What do you need to do to give your team members the flexibility to deliver the expected results in creative ways?

Today I will…

Stop Delegating on a Whim

If you aren't crystal clear about what and why you are delegating, it is better to do it yourself. Random delegation usually yields poor results and may end up costing you in the end.

Today I will…

-137-

Become a Priority Expert

By using the 1-4 priority code system you will get clear about
what needs to get done: 1=today; 2=this week; 3=this month;
4=this quarter or ongoing. Assign a number to each of your to-
do tasks and check
for patterns.

Today I will...

Zap Excuses

What are some of the most common or interesting excuses you hear from your team members? Here are some of ours: "I'm on it." "They are getting back to me about it." "My computer crashed." Zap the ones you hear consistently by clarifying your expectations and outline action steps for change.

Today I will...

-139-

Get Organized

Take a look at your desk and organize at least one folder, pile, or drawer to get more clarity about your work. When we have physical clutter around us, we
tend to get mentally overwhelmed.

Today I will...

−140−

Rethink Your Approach

Consider at least one other strategy or approach you can use with your team members to get them more engaged and motivated to take the initiative.

Today I will…

–141–

Today I'm Ready For...

Complete the sentence above, focusing on the positive actions, thoughts, and behaviors you want to embrace today.

Today I'm ready for...

Connect With a Quote

"One of the most important tasks of a manager is to eliminate his people's excuses for failure."

– Robert Townsend

What excuses do you need to address?

Today I will...

−143−

Take a Break

Take a 15-mintue break and leave the office. If possible, get some fresh air and walk around outside. When you return, notice whether you have more clarity and focus.

Today I will…

–144–

Connect With a Colleague

Your colleagues serve many important roles. Ask one of them out to lunch to connect on challenges and discuss opportunities. Pick each other's brains by asking questions about how to handle specific situations.

Today I will...

–145–

Thank Someone

Thank at least one other person this week. We often forget to be thankful for the nice things that take place. It will offer you an opportunity to be positive and inspired.

Today I will…

Consider Your Successor

Who will take your place when you are ready to move on? If you don't know, spend 15 minutes today considering your options and the action steps needed to replace you in the future.

Today I will…

−147−

Create a Future File

Think of yourself in your ideal future. What will you be doing? How are you working and with whom? Write a short paragraph as if you are already in that future describing what you are doing and how you are feeling. Keep these notes in a file titled, "Future File" and refer to it once a month.

Today I will...

-148-

Today I'm Ready For...

Complete the sentence above, focusing on the positive actions, thoughts, and behaviors you want to embrace today.

Today I'm ready for...

−149−

Connect With a Quote

"Successful managers don't wait for an appraisal to offer feedback to employees that improves their performance."

– Jessika Magnusson

Whom can you give feedback to today ?
What will help him or her be successful?

Today I will…

-150-

Are You Inspiring Anyone?

If you don't know or don't think so, what changes do you need to make to be a manager who inspires others to reach their full potential? If you are, how do you tap into it?

Today I will...

–151–

Give Feedback Continuously

Great managers offer feedback frequently, and they have learned to deliver both positive and critical information. When handled effectively, feedback can be a powerful motivator.

Today I will...

Step Outside Your Comfort Zone

Giving feedback (even positive) can make even the most easygoing manager uncomfortable. Step outside your comfort zone and offer feedback to your team members.

Today I will...

–153–

Know Your Feedback Needs

You may need more or less feedback than others. Audit yourself and consider how much feedback you need. Meet with your manager to discuss and agree on a feedback system that works for you.

Today I will…

-154-

Know Your Peeps' Feedback Needs

Ask your team to share their feedback needs with you. Set up meetings to give them what they need.

Today I will...

–155–

Today I'm Ready For...

Complete the sentence above, focusing on the positive actions, thoughts, and behaviors you want to embrace today.

Today I'm ready for...

Connect With a Quote

"There are two differing approaches ,and they have different virtues, the method of talent management and recruitment."

– John Gibbons

Whose talents do you need to manage?
Whose talents do you need to hire?

Today I will…

−157−

Spend Your Time Wisely

Audit how you are spending your management time. How much of your time is spent giving feedback, rewarding, and coaching others? If it is less than 10 percent, aim to increase it by at least 30 minutes
this week.

Today I will...

Check in on
Performance Goals

It is easy to forget to monitor the goals you set for the year.
Make it a habit to connect once a month with your team
members to see how your goals are progressing.

Today I will…

−159−

Check in on Your Own Goals

How are you progressing? Are you spending time developing your own skills? If you want more progress, set aside one hour this week to focus on your own personal and professional development.

Today I will...

–160–

Polish Your Coaching Skills

To coach is to help others find their own answers and ask powerful questions to help them move into action. Check to see if you are asking open-ended vs. close-ended questions. To make sure they are open-ended, start questions with "how," "what," "when," and "where."

Today I will…

Today I'm Ready For...

Complete the sentence above, focusing on the positive actions, thoughts, and behaviors you want to embrace today.

Today I'm ready for...

Connect With a Quote

*"If you set out to be liked, you would be prepared
to compromise on anything at any time,
and you would achieve nothing."*

– Margaret Thatcher

What fear do you need to let go of
in order to make sure that you don't get stuck
in the "wanting to be liked" trap?

Today I will…

-163-

Don't Get Hung Up on Personalities

When giving feedback, focus on behaviors, not personalities.
Offer specific and detailed feedback
that your team members can use.

Today I will...

-164-

It's Not About You

It's easy to begin feeling like the world revolves around us at times. When we coach others, we need to remember that it isn't about us; it's about them. By staying objective, we are much more powerful as coaches.

Today I will...

–165–

To Manage, Lead, or Coach? That's the Question

Different circumstances require different interventions. Manage processes, lead people, and coach to increase awareness and action. Check to see if you are using the right strategy for the right occasion.

Today I will…

-166-

Volunteer Your Help

Ask a colleague, boss, or team member if there is anything you can do to help today. Let them know that you have 15-30 minutes of time and ask what they may need. The more you put out there, the more you
get back.

Today I will...

–167–

Make a BIG List

Use flip-chart-sized paper and write down at least five big goals for your team. Put it visibly in your office and invite your team in. Encourage them to connect their goals to yours, so you see them every day.

Today I will…

-168-

Today I'm Ready For...

Complete the sentence above, focusing on the positive actions, thoughts, and behaviors you want to embrace today.

Today I'm ready for...

Connect With a Quote

*"I can do things you cannot; you can do things I cannot; together
we can do great things."*

– Mother Teresa

Who can you team up with to get more things done
and maximize each other's strengths?

Today I will...

–170–

Tap Into Your Drivers

Get motivated by doing one thing that you are truly passionate about for at least one hour today. Check your productivity afterward. What did you accomplish and with what level of effort?

Today I will...

–171–

Do Something Fun Together

Schedule a half-day session outside the office for team building and team syncing. Take a cooking class or do a volunteer project together. The energy you build within the team will carry through for weeks.

Today I will…

-172-

Sticky Note It!

Write a message to yourself on a small sticky note and place it where you see it every day. It can be an affirmation or inspirational message. The key is to look at it every day to encourage your personal and professional growth.

Today I will...

–173–

Get in Touch With Your Passions

When we are passionate about what we do, we tap into all sorts of emotions and produce extraordinary results. Ask yourself what you are passionate about. Then review your work and see how many of your daily activities tap into your deep passions. If most don't, what do you need to change, modify, or create in order to be more aligned?

Today I will…

Today I'm Ready For...

Complete the sentence above, focusing on the
positive actions, thoughts, and behaviors you want
to embrace today.

Today I'm ready for...

Connect With a Quote

*"When people engage in conflict, it means they care,
and the topic of the conflict truly matters to them."*

– Jessika Magnusson

What questions do you need to ask yourself and your
team to uncover what truly matters
to you during conflicting situations?

Today I will…

–176–

Embrace Your Dark Side

We all have "shadow behaviors," and they tend to show up under stress. List at least one shadow that you are aware of displaying under stress. Write it on a sticky note and keep it where you can see it every day. List one strategy for managing it more effectively in preparation for its reappearance.

Today I will...

–177–

Recognize Conflict
As a Catalyst

Conflict can be a powerful catalyst for change and creativity. Check in with your natural response to conflict. Do you avoid it? Do you confront things head-on? Do you pretend conflict doesn't exist? Do you wait to see what happens? Does your response help or hurt the team?

Today I will…

Control Your Emotions

You can't control how you feel, but you can control the emotional response you exude. Some people wear their emotions on their sleeves, and some put them aside and aren't able to use them effectively to inspire others. Rank yourself on a scale from 1-10 (1 being poorly, 10 being extremely well) on how you use emotions to tap into your team's motivators.

Today I will...

−179−

Read the Intensity

Conflicts have different levels of intensity. When someone comes to you for help resolving a conflict, can you accurately determine the true intensity, or do you tend to over- or under-estimate it and rely on the emotions of the people involved? Next time you have the opportunity to assist, stay neutral and attempt to objectively determine the intensity level.

Today I will...

-180-

Today I'm Ready For...

Complete the sentence above, focusing on the
positive actions, thoughts, and behaviors you want
to embrace today.

Today I'm ready for...

-181-

Be Aware of Conflict Signs

Most conflicts don't exist in a vacuum. There are usually signs well ahead of the conflict that can be addressed to prevent disastrous results. Watch for some of these common signs: Eye-rolling in meetings, overt sarcasm, direct attacks on others, and gossiping.

Today I will...

Connect With a Quote

"Conflict is the beginning of consciousness."

– M. Esther Harding

What clarity can conflict bring to you?

Today I will…

-183-

Nip Destructive Behaviors in the Bud

To create an effective team environment, commit to addressing and resolving destructive behaviors immediately. Let the affected persons know that you don't tolerate these types of behaviors and will take action should they occur. Set the tone for your team by being a strong manager.

Today I will...

Clarify Your Standards
and Expectations

You make it a lot easier on your people if you clearly state how you want conflicts to be addressed. Create a standard for resolving conflicts effectively and share it with your team.

Today I will…

–185–

Address What Makes You Uncomfortable

Set aside 10 minutes today to consider what situations, people, and actions make you uncomfortable. Pick one scenario that you want to address and meet with that person to discuss the issue today.

Today I will…

Ask For Help

If you don't utilize this underused strategy, it can lead to burnout and loss of creativity. Today, ask one person to help you with a project or to brainstorm solutions to a challenge you haven't been able to resolve. Notice the positive feelings that come with collaborating.

Today I will...

–187–

Today I'm Ready For...

Complete the sentence above, focusing on the
positive actions, thoughts, and behaviors you want
to embrace today.

Today I'm ready for...

Connect With a Quote

"Worry gives a small thing a big shadow."

– Swedish proverb

What are you worrying about today? What do you need to do to move past worrying and into action? What do you need to let go?

Today I will...

DAY

-189-

Visualize Your
Perfect Mentor

Set aside 30 minutes to write down the characteristics that you
most admire in a person (personally or professionally). List the
characteristics of an ideal mentor, not worrying if such a person
exists. Review
the list and begin to think of people who may match
the list closely.

Today I will...

Seek Out Your Perfect Mentor

Mentors can be living or dead; they can live close or far away. A mentor is someone you admire and someone who inspires you to be your best. Study that person and, if possible, seek her out. If the individual is no longer around, research how she lived and worked and commit to emulating some of her behaviors and values.

Today I will...

-191-

Get a Coach

A coach is someone you hire to be your unconditionally supportive, challenging, and honest advisor. If you are ready to grow and develop, and if you feel that you need more support than you currently have, hiring a coach may be a great idea.

Today I will...

Coach Your Peeps

It's easy to get lost doing the work, while forgetting to set aside time to coach and train your people. Set aside 30 minutes on each team member's schedule to coach them on how to get better results. Use coachlike questions that start with, "What," "When," "Where," and "How."

Today I will...

−193−

Stop Asking Why

If you get trapped in asking too many "why" questions, you limit your opportunities to go deeper to get real answers. Stop asking why and replace it with "What," "When," "Where," and "How" instead.

Today I will...

Today I'm Ready For...

Complete the sentence above, focusing on the
positive actions, thoughts, and behaviors you want
to embrace today.

Today I'm ready for...

-195-

Connect With a Quote

"Don't wish it were easier, wish you were better."

– Jim Rohn

What traits do you need to develop in order to become better at what you do?

Today I will…

Be the Change You Seek

Commit to changing one thing about yourself or your environment in order to create positive results today. When we focus on changing others, we can become judgmental and negative. Start from the inside and work your way out.

Today I will...

DAY

–197–

Set Aside YOU Time

Set aside 45 minutes this week to focus on what you want.
Consider what you want to do professionally and what you wish
your could do personally. Create one small action step to move
yourself in that direction.

Today I will…

Set Aside BOSS Time

Schedule 15 minutes to consider what you can do for your boss today. Approach him or her and ask what you can do or suggest an action step that you think may be helpful. This strategy will yield positive karma for months, if not years.

Today I will...

Learn to Follow

As managers and leaders, we are counted upon to inspire and move others in a predetermined direction. For today, consider what it would take to be a great follower. Remain active and engaged without telling others what to do.

Today I will...

Practice Flawless Followership

You are not born a natural leader, and you are not born a natural follower. It takes practice. The four key concepts of "followership" include being grounded, connected, open, and active. Which of these four concepts do you need to develop in order to follow
more effectively?

Today I will…

−201−

Today I'm Ready For...

Complete the sentence above, focusing on the positive actions, thoughts, and behaviors you want to embrace today.

Today I'm ready for...

Connect With a Quote

*"You gain strength, courage and confidence
by every experience in which you must stop
and look fear in the face."*

– Eleanor Roosevelt

What experiences are you avoiding because
you are afraid or unsure? What are the costs to you
or the organization of doing so?

Today I will…

−203−

Feel the Fear

We sometimes forget to acknowledge what scares us. Maybe it is asking for a promotion, addressing poor performance from a team member, or setting boundaries with peers. The first step in moving past our fears is to feel the fear and recognize that it's there. Do nothing more with it today.

Today I will...

Create Action Steps
That Rock

Sometimes we get overly comfortable, and we need to challenge ourselves to reach new levels. Create one action step today that forces you outside your comfort zone. Record the perceived rewards of stepping outside the box.

Today I will…

-205-

Rock Your Steps

Once you have at least one radical action step created, act on it. What results did you experience? How did it feel to think and act big?

Today I will...

–206–

Disconnect Regularly

Most of us are so connected and plugged in that we don't know how to disconnect to recharge. Today, set aside at least 10 minutes to be disconnected from it all (including smart phones, mobile devices, and computers). Give your creative thoughts a chance
to blossom.

Today I will…

-207-

Plan a Quiet Vacation

Most of us plan vacations to recharge and get away, yet we bring our laptops and insist on responding to emails. Plan a vacation or a long weekend where you will have quiet time and will not respond to the requests of others.

Today I will...

-208-

Celebrate Your Awesomeness

Take yourself out for lunch or coffee today to celebrate how awesome you are! Chances are, everyone else is too busy to do it for you.

Today I will...

-209-

Today I'm Ready For...

Complete the sentence above, focusing on the
positive actions, thoughts, and behaviors you want
to embrace today.

Today I'm ready for...

Connect With a Quote

"Try to relax and enjoy the crisis."

– Ashleigh Brilliant

What do you need to relax about or let go of
in order to just go with the flow?

Today I will…

−211−

Make a Difference

Commit to doing something today that makes a difference. It can be for your team, your peers, your boss, or a complete stranger. When we focus on activities that matter, we tap into our motivation.

Today I will...

Fix a Recurring Problem

We sometimes get too busy to fix things that recur over and over again, zapping our time and talents. Get rid of at least one recurring issue today and watch your energy soar.

Today I will...

DAY
−213−

Focus for 15

Set aside 15 minutes today for uninterrupted focusing. Remove all distractions (set phone to go to voice mail, turn off the wireless on your computer, and turn off the cellphone). Set an alarm that rings when the time is up, and see how much work you get done.

Today I will…

Be Early for All Meetings

Showing up on time is good. Showing up early communicates that you value and respect other people's time and resources. Make it a habit today or for the rest of the week to show up early. Notice how being early contributes to your focus, preparedness, and ability to connect with others.

Today I will...

−215−

Request a Confirmation

Next time you email a new person or contact, request an email confirmation to ensure that your messages won't end up in spam or the company's screening system. This prevents any unnecessary miscommunications or excuses.

Today I will...

Today I'm Ready For...

Complete the sentence above, focusing on the positive actions, thoughts, and behaviors you want to embrace today.

Today I'm ready for…

Connect With a Quote

*"True leadership must be for the benefit of the followers,
not the enrichment of the leaders."*

– Robert Townsend

How would your team benefit if you
sharpened your leadership and management skills?

Today I will…

DAY
-218-

Throw a
"Lunch is on Me" Party

There are few things as powerful as free lunch parties. Make it a
habit to show your appreciation by taking the team or individual
team members out to lunch once a quarter. Make it random and
impromptu.

Today I will…

Give the Gift of Time

If you are able to, offer your team members incentives for getting things done sooner, while maintaining a focus on quality. Give them an extra hour off for lunch, or let them go home early as a reward for going above and beyond on a specific task.

Today I will…

Follow Through

For each activity you commit to today, follow through flawlessly. If you can't get it done today, tell the person requesting your time that you won't be able to deliver today and offer an alternative date/time.

Today I will…

DAY

−221−

And the Theme Is…

Create a theme for the year or month. Use it with your team to remind you what is most important.

Today I will…

What Are Your Filler Words?

If you are prone to filling in sentences you speak with "uhm," "like," and "you know," make a commitment to stop using these filler words. Coming across as a polished communicator is imperative to being a
great manager.

Today I will…

-223-

Today I'm Ready For...

Complete the sentence above, focusing on the positive actions, thoughts, and behaviors you want to embrace today.

Today I'm ready for...

−224−

Be Transparent

Let your people know what you are working on, what your challenges are, and how they can help. Transparent managers are more engaged, work more effectively with others, and get more done.

Today I will...

-225-

Be Curious

Ask your team deeper questions about their work or processes.
Be curious about how they do things and how they use their
talents effectively.

Today I will...

Connect With a Quote

"Leadership needs to spend more time, effort and resources at all levels to redefine what it is that people really need to thrive today."

– Leslie Murphy

How much time will you set aside to investigate what people need in order to thrive in their jobs/careers?

Today I will…

DAY
−227−

Be in on the Hip
and Happening

You don't have to be cool and trendy to know what is going on in the world. Take a break and surf the latest news or look up a resource that offers insight into your content-matter expertise. It's easy to make connections with others when you have something interesting to talk about.

Today I will…

Write an Article

You don't have to be a literary genius to put together a short 300- to 500-word article about something you are great at or feel passionate about. Set aside 30 minutes today to map out a concept or general outline.

Today I will...

-229-

Read an Article

Do you have piles of articles or magazines on your desk? If so, pick one magazine at random, select one article that catches your attention, set aside 30 minutes to read it, then recycle the rest of the resource. You only need to get one good concept from each resource to get its value.

Today I will…

-230-

Today I'm Ready For...

Complete the sentence above, focusing on the positive actions, thoughts, and behaviors you want to embrace today.

Today I'm ready for...

Share a Resource

Review the magazines or online resources you intend to go through someday, look for an article or piece of information that would be helpful to someone else (client, boss, peer, team member), and forward it. Notice the response from the recipient.

Today I will...

Connect With a Quote

"Our best thoughts come from others."

– Ralph Waldo Emerson

What are some of the best thoughts you
have received from another person?
How have they influenced what you are doing now?

Today I will...

DAY
-233-

Ask Someone to Share

Connect with your resource-happy peers and ask them to share something they do or use that helps them be effective managers.

Today I will...

How Open Are You?

Practice using this opening sentence when you need to offer someone critical feedback. You may modify it by saying, "Is now a good time to give you some tough feedback?" Ask permission before you barge in and begin sharing. First make sure the person is receptive.

Today I will...

-235-

"Today's Gonna Be a Good Good Day"

Make the decision to turn any obstacle or challenge in to an opportunity today. An unwaveringly positive attitude is contagious, and it will inspire others to move from feeling stuck to exploring possibilities.

Today I will...

-236-

Place a Spotlight on Your Work

Highlight something you do really well today, and let the proverbial spotlight highlight your talents. You can do so without bragging or bravado. Simply state or share something you are great at, and inspire others to do the same.

Today I will...

-237-

Today I'm Ready For...

Complete the sentence above, focusing on the positive actions, thoughts, and behaviors you want to embrace today.

Today I'm ready for...

Connect With a Quote

*"We are what we repeatedly do.
Excellence, then, is not an act, but a habit."*

–Aristotle

What would you like to do repeatedly in order
to develop excellence?

Today I will...

-239-

Rinse and Repeat

If you implemented or acted on at least one of the tips in the book, you have already improved your management skills significantly. If you shared one of these resources with someone else, you offered the organization and your team tremendous value. Now go back and do it again! To create new and powerful habits, we need to practice over and over to make them stick.

Today I will...

−240−

The Most Powerful Change
I Made...

Record the most powerful change you made, thanks to using this book. Record how it has helped, what changes you were able to make as a result, and the measurable outcomes you have experienced. Share the news with your manager or team members, and encourage them to work at their craft each day.

Today I will...

About the Author

Jessika Magnusson is a master-level, award-winning executive coach. She is best known for sharing her leadership and management expertise utilizing her "no frills no fluff" method, which consistently produces measurable, sustainable results to corporations and their leaders around the globe. Jessika delivers her management message in a straightforward, honest, direct and supportive way, which gets to the heart of each individual matter quickly and efficiently.

In her latest book, Jessika shares daily, bite-size tips that deal with the challenges of management. Each tip is meant to be contemplated individually, one each day, to allow the reader to process and implement the information. From dealing with wishy-washy goal-setting to rewarding yourself for stretching your management skills, you will find that committing yourself to following these 240 tips will transform you into a more effective and grounded manager!

Jessika, a native of Sweden, holds a master's degree in instructional design from Johnson & Wales University in Providence, RI. Her global leadership consulting company, Leadership Cadence, is located in Los Angeles, CA with an office in Dubai, UAE.

She is also a champion amateur ballroom dancer, and in 2011 launched Next Level Dancing, LLC, a company, which offers Jessika's unique coaching style to the ballroom dance world. In her books, *The Ballroom Dance Coach* and *Competing Like a Pro*, she offers the same "no frills no fluff" advice to dancers who want to take their skills to the next level.